FRANK PRYKE
PROSPECTOR

—

HANK NELSON

With Two Stories by Ion Idriess

ETT IMPRINT

Exile Bay

First published by ETT Imprint, Exile Bay in 2020

A much abbreviated version of this text appeared first as Frank Pryke: Prospector' in *Papua New Guinea Portraits: The Expatriate Experience*, edited by James Griffin, pp. 75–100. Canberra: ANU Press.

ETT IMPRINT
PO Box R1906

Royal Exchange NSW 1225
Australia

ISBN 978-1-922384-18-8 (paper)
ISBN 978-1-922384-19-5 (ebook)

Text designed by Hanna Gotlieb
Cover and internal design by Tom Thompson
Photographs courtesy of ETT Imprint, Pictorial Press, the National Library of Australia and the PAMBU collection.

Frank Pryke in Sydney 1933.

Koiari Treehouse by Charles Kerry 1913.

CONTENTS

By the time Frank Pryke's ashes were buried at Samarai in 1937 there was little of Papua New Guinea he had not seen in his search for gold. He, more than any other, could have confirmed the miners' lore: 'There's gold in New Guinea but there's a lot of New Guinea mixed with it'. Thoughtful, humane, energetic and tough, Pryke tried a number of occupations, tanner, publican, billiard saloon proprietor, fancy goods salesman and newsagent in a country town, and suburban storekeeper; but he always returned to prospecting, and it was as a prospector that his determination, restlessness and bushmanship gave him success. Among the small group of men who mined gold in British New Guinea, German New Guinea, Papua, and Australian New Guinea he alone made a candid record of what he saw, and much of his writing has survived.

Born in 1872 the son of a miner from near Sofala on the old Turon gold fields of New South Wales, Frank Pryke served his time as a tanner in Goulburn[1]. Having failed to find work in his trade in Goulburn and New Zealand, Frank returned to Sydney where he met his brother Dan just back from prospecting on the Murchison and Coolgardie gold fields of Western Australia. Frank and Dan went back to Western Australia with Dan prospecting around Lake Darlot in treacherously dry country 300 miles north of Kalgoorlie. After some success at a place called Pryke's Eucalyptus near Brummer Creek , the brothers decided to try their luck on McLachlan's Creek on the upper Mambare in New Guinea.

Gold had first been mined in New Guinea in 1888 when about 400 north Queensland diggers worked shallow alluvial deposits in Sudest Island in the Louisiade Archipelago. In 1889 the diggers moved to the neighbouring island of Misima. The island gold fields were kept alive by another strike at Woodlark in 1895, and in the next year gold was found on the

Papuan natives 1900.

mainland, in MacLaughlin's Creek on the upper Mambare. In spite of stories of savage blacks, poisoned arrows and lurking fevers, nearly 1000 miners sailed to New Guinea in 1896 and 1897. About 400 of them landed in Port Moresby.

Without money and stores most found it impossible to reach the gold fields of the Northern Division. Twelve of those who attempted to cross overland to MacLaughlin's Creek died either on the track or in Port Moresby. Only two parties reached the Mambare by land and they suffered terrible privations on what MacGregor thought should have been a fifteen day walk for those accustomed to travel in New Guinea. By the end of 1896 there were only about twelve men on MacLaughlin's Creek and they were getting little gold. But in 1895 MacGregor had ascended the Musa, taking with him six stranded prospectors. They had found traces of gold and MacGregor reported that the upper Musa would 'present a fine field for the prospector'.[2] Following MacGregor's advice W. Simpson and W. McLelland prospected on the Moni, a branch of the Musa, further signs of gold had been found towards the end of 1896.

By the time Dan and Frank Pryke arrived in Samarai it must have been known that those miners who went to MacLaughlin's Creek faced a difficult track and on reaching the upper Mambare had little chance of obtaining either gold or stores. The earlier fields on Misima and Sudest were almost deserted and, while there was gold on Woodlark, the area was over-manned. The Prykes and ten other prospectors therefore took the schooner Ellengowan to Normanby and Fergusson Islands where they recruited carriers to follow Simpson and McLelland up the Musa. It was, Frank wrote, 'a terrible job getting up, took seven weeks' and when they were about seventy miles up the river the 'boys' ran away. Frank and four others pressed on up the Moni but found no gold. Trying to raft downstream

Frank was caught in rapids, tossed into the water and washed downstream: 'I was three days and a half making my way back to main camp and all that time without food of any kind and nearly pegged out'. Frank recovered after a fortnight's rest in camp and joined the party for the trip to the coast where they found a letter left for them from Matthew Moreton, the Resident Magistrate, telling them that John Green and his police had been killed on the Mambare.[3] After an eighteen day wait on the beach they were picked up in March 1897 by a passing cutter. The expedition broke up, Dan and Frank going on to Bartle Bay, a small gold field opened in 1894, just to the east of Dogura. After three months on the Magavara River they made

their way by canoe and cutter to Samarai where they boarded a schooner for Cooktown. Frank tried the alluvial field on the Starcke River in North Queensland for a month before going south to Cairns and the rain forests of the Russell Creek field. He 'stayed there about eight months. Done no good so then carried swag down to Jordan Creek rush'.

Having recovered his health in Sydney Frank was back in British New Guinea by 1899 or 1900. In partnership with George Klotz he recruited labourers and went up the Mambare, disembarking at Tamata, a place known to all the miners for its government station, Whitten Brothers' store, bloody clashes with the Binandere people, and malaria. Crossing to the Gira, Pryke and Klotz had a look at Elliott's Creek where gold had been found in 1897 and then climbed the divide to the Chirima, a tributary of the Mambare. Using knives, handkerchiefs, matches, plane iron and beads for trade, they purchased a pig, sweet potatoes, pumpkins, taro and bananas from the local villagers. Pryke noted that the people 'seemed very glad that we had come amongst them as they appeared to have lived in great dread of one another'.[4]

Papuans 1900, and below, the famous Combined Goulburn Rugby Union Club that beat the Sydney Premiers Glebe in 1900, this one featuring three Prykes (Jim Pryke top right), with both Frank and Dan having left the team to explore Papua New Guinea.

Confirming judgments made by others, Pryke wrote that the Chirima people were 'most friendly' and he contrasted them with the Orokaivas who, he said, were 'known and dreaded' because they had murdered and eaten a great many carriers since MacLaughlin's Creek had been found. Accompanied by thirty men from Beda village in the Chirima Valley carrying sweet potato, Pryke and Klotz went down the Chirima and then up the Mambare to join a new rush to Finnigan's Creek on the Yodda gold field.

About thirty men were already camped on the field 'nearly starving' as the last lot of tucker which came out only ran to one and a half pounds of flour, two tins of meat per man'. During the first year it was worked, 6000 ounces were taken from Finnigan's and neighbouring creeks, but one-third of the miners and their labourers died.[5] Pryke and Klotz 'did fairly well' on the Yodda 'getting 85 ounces per man' and only left when their labourers' contracts ran out.[6] Returning, they came down the old MacLaughlin's Creek track to Tamata. 'It is a terrible road for boys to carry loads on', Frank wrote, 'I am not surprised that boys who have been there dread to hear the name of Mambare mentioned'. After they paid off their labourers in front of the resident magistrate in Samarai, Klotz bought a cutter which they used to return their men home. At Gabagabuna on Milne Bay Klotz and Pryke recruited their health on 'fowl and fish and occasional blowouts on pig'.

With six carriers Pryke and Klotz left Gabagabuna in March 1901 and went overland to Bartle Bay. Sick with malaria, hampered by rain and able to obtain little food from local villagers, they prospected the rivers at the back of Topura and Wedau before crossing the divide back to Milne Bay. In April they left Samarai for Cloudy Bay where a party of prospectors had reported a small find. Six days after anchoring the cutter in one

Samarai in 1900.

of the streams flowing into the bay, Frank washed two and a half penny-weights in a ravine. Deciding it was worth working, they shifted camp onto the gully and put in a sluice-box. For the rest of May and June they washed up to twelve ounces a day. Adding to their stores by dynamiting streams for fish and sending the labourers out to trade with local villagers for potatoes, taros and yams, Pryke and Klotz worked the ravine until the middle of July, when they left with 370 ounces.

In Samarai another experienced miner, George Arnold,[7] joined the partners for their return to Cloudy Bay. On their second trip they found the anchorage crowded with cutters, a store established on the shore and about thirty men on the field. They found little gold. The ravine had sheltered a concentrated patch and it was soon worked out. Klotz, Arnold and Pryke stayed only two weeks, getting about twenty ounces before they left to prospect to the northeast of Robinson River. But after a fortnight they returned to the cutter and, using it as a base, tested the creeks between Cloudy Bay and Samarai.

Dan Pryke, who had an interest in a reefing lease on Woodlark, joined Frank and Klotz for another attempt to find gold at the head of the Musa in 1902. Klotz decided to go trading in his cutter and left the prospectors before they struck gold in the Keveri Valley.[8]

Ironically the new field was just over the Owen Stanley Range from Cloudy Bay, not far from where the Prykes had prospected on the upper tributaries of the Musa on their first trip to British New Guinea in 1897. After a 'sweet climb' over the range the miners looked down on about forty square miles of rolling grasslands cut by sharp spurs and swift flowing streams. At an altitude of 2000 feet Keveri was cool, healthy and remote. It was 'happy valley'.[9]

Frank returned to Keveri with Dan in 1903 and 1904 and

with Jim, a younger brother, in 1905. Each year they left Samarai in a small boat and recruited around Normanby and Fergusson Islands and Milne Bay. Often they returned to villages where they were known and signed on men who had worked for them before. If the villagers were engaged in a 'Christmas' the Prykes might take three to four weeks to find men willing to recruit. In Samarai the labourers were examined by the medical officer and then the resident magistrate witnessed the signing on, each man having a cross put next to his name on the form, which noted his home village and that he had agreed to work for £1 a month carrying and mining at Cloudy Bay. Jim was so impressed with the work of Dr R. Fleming Jones, who occasionally rejected one of their recruits, that he paid him tribute in verse:[10]

When you've been on holiday
To the Trobriands or the bay
Call and see Jones M.D.
Buxom, bright New Guinea ladies
Give your constitution Hades
If you want to seem a saint
Clear of syphilitic taint
Don't be a dunce — consult at once
Jones M.D.

With their 'team' of twelve or twenty labourers and basic stores for twelve months, the Prykes took a boat down to Cloudy Bay and established a base at Ganai.[11] From Ganai, the labourers made frequent trips carrying supplies into Keveri Valley where the Prykes panned or boxed wherever they found payable alluvial. Frank, who was unable to 'suffer setting in on five or six dwts a day',[12] was often out prospecting.

In December 1905 he spent a month with Fred Kruger testing the country along the Adau, Domora and Moni Rivers. The greatest number of white miners at Keveri at any one time was about fifteen and they employed 100 labourers.[13] During 1905 there were only four other miners in the valley. From the constant movement of the miners the Prykes picked up news: that most of the men on the Gira were in debt, that old Steve Woolf 'had been sentenced to death for murder of a nigger'[14] but his sentence had been reduced to three years' jail and that Delaney 'was going out to the Trobriands to get a wife to bring back with him'.[15] When the labourer's time had expired the Prykes picked up a boat if one was available at Cloudy Bay. If not, they walked or took a small canoe to Mailu where there was a chance of obtaining a bigger canoe for the trip into Samarai.

At the end of 1903 Dan went to Cooktown and deposited 256 ounces of gold with the Bank of North Queensland. Frank stayed in Samarai where the complete entry in his diary for 8 November was 'imbibing'. He recovered to play cricket at Kwato next day.

The Prykes took 190 ounces to Samarai in 1904 and 213 in May 1906. Both Frank and Dan were able to take trips to southern Australia at the end of 1904 and, when Dan decided to leave New Guinea to become a husband and the proprietor of the Royal Exchange Hotel, Armidale, he was able to declare to his fiancee that his total assets after five years in New Guinea were £400 in a bank in Cooktown, a £250 share in a Cairns ice-works and a Woodlark lease, which he eventually sold for £130. He also admitted: 'I have thrown away a lot of money in my life'.[16]

When the Prykes went to Keveri in 1904 they took with them Luke Soich an old miner who had worked with Dan on

Frank Pryke's photograph of their regular transport, a lakatoi or motu trading vessel, 1905..

Woodlark[17] Soon after they began work on the field a stone thrown out by dynamite used to cut a race smashed Soich's leg above the knee. Dan and Frank put his leg in splints. Having sent one man to the coast to hold any boat that might be in the area, the Prykes and a troop of labourers set out to carry Soich to the coast. 'Coming down the main range today', Dan wrote' it looked impossible to carry a man on a stretcher but the boys were really splendid.' On the third day they had reached Ganai where a boat was waiting. Dan accompanied Soich to Samarai and the doctor amputated the leg but old Luke died a few hours later.

In 1901 people speaking the Bauwaki language lived in small fortified villages on ridge tops near the Mori to the west of Cloudy Bay, along the headwaters of the Gadoguina River and across the ranges into the Keveri Valley and to Mt Suckling in the north-east.[18]

People speaking the Binahari language lived on the Robinson River, and on the coast close to Cloudy Bay were Morawa speakers. All three languages were related to Mailu, the major language of the south coast. But in other obvious characteristics of their culture, particularly in the wearing of long pig tails wound in bark, the Keveri showed associations with people to the north. By 1901 they knew of the government but were not under government control. One patrol[19] had crossed the valley and other patrols had demonstrated government power among their neighbours on the north, west and south. Foreigners who entered the area spoke of the frequency of death by violence among the Keveri. Warfare involving large numbers of warriors was unusual; the quick raid by a small group to kill one or two victims was known. After spending a boring six weeks in the Keveri valley in 1940, F.E. Williams, the government anthropologist, concluded that 'whatever the cause, there can be no doubt that the salient feature of the Keveri... was nothing other than an intense interest in killing.'[20]

When the Prykes entered the area they employed people from the coast as carriers and used Keveri men as guides on prospecting trips. They encouraged the Keveri to bring in food for sale: if food was scarce in the gardens all suffered. In addition, the 'gun boys' combed the surrounding country shooting wallabies, cassowaries, birds and wild pigs. On a Sunday Frank Pryke often 'shot' (dynamited) fish.

Generally the Keveri peoples offered little resistance to the miners who occupied their lands. But they continued their own feuds, which were complicated by the movement of local men employed by miners and by the arrival of labourers from distant areas.

The violence reached its height in 1903-4, when fifteen indentured labourers who had absconded from the Keveri gold field were killed either as they left the valley or along the coast.[21] In their diaries the Prykes record no desertions of their men, but they could not avoid some involvement in the conflicts around them. Their carriers, particularly those from Ganai village near the head of Cloudy Bay, were in danger when they took stores into Keveri.

The Prykes knew many of the Keveri as individuals; when Frank and Jim returned in 1905 Frank wrote to Dan speaking of their friendly reunion in the valley and how the villagers had asked after Dan.[22] A.C. English after he visited the area in 1904 wrote that 'the miners all get along first rate with the natives' and the Prykes in particular were 'held in high esteem.'[23] There was very little thieving from camps which had angered miners in other areas, although on one occasion Frank helped Delaney set a gun trap and afterwards when he saw the victim 'going for his natural' he was delighted to think of him spending hours picking gravel from himself.[24]

Not long before the Prykes left the area in 1906 a Ganai man was speared and tomahawked to death.[25] One of the Prykes' Milne Bay labourers said that the Keveri people had previously threatened the man when he carried a swag into Keveri: they accused him of having been on a raid to Keveri and killing one of their 'chiefs'. Two months later the Prykes were told that the Barua people had attempted to spear the carriers as they crossed the ranges and their 'gun boys' had killed three of them. One man employed by the Prykes and another employed by Kruger were arrested and taken for trial to Port Moresby. Kruger, angry with the government's interference, wanted to go to Port Moresby to defend them, but Frank opposed the idea, contenting himself with making a statement to Hubert Murray, then chief judicial officer, in Samarai that the Barua had been 'causing a lot of trouble down that way for some time past'.[26]

In Port Moresby the two arrested men said that no spears had been thrown at them and they were sentenced to death, then reprieved.

While at Keveri Frank Pryke had seen little of the government. Officially proclaimed a gold field in 1904 only, Keveri had no resident warden. Albert English, the Government Agent and later Assistant Resident Magistrate at Rigo, divided his time between his private trading, planting and government business and could do little about the distant Abau area. In any case the government parties were usually unwelcome, partly because they forced the people out of the valley and cut off the miners' source of fresh food. Frank also thought they did little to keep the peace. He wrote to Dan on 13 October 1905, while English was in the valley attempting to arrest some Keveri men responsible for a raid on a village close to Cloudy Bay:

We have had a bit of excitement here this last week. English is here with a detachment of police and a mob of carriers chivvying these people around. He has captured six prisoners and shot ten pigs and has been feeding his mob on the gardens.

In his report English admitted that the miners would have been happier if the government had stayed away. In another letter to Dan (5 March 1906), Frank made a more general comment on the government's infrequent attempts to change the way of life of the Keveri:

. . . I think that their way of civilizing the niggers is all at sea, and an impossible kind of way of doing it. I think that they should either leave them alone to settle their own feuds or else when they start out to give them a lesson they should give them a proper one, and not make a farce of it by taking a few harmless ones who are either too old or too young to be in the mischief and giving them a few months or a few years while the real culprits almost invariably escape.

Besides this the white officials are greatly handicapped by the crude material with which they have to do their civilizing. Fancy starting out to civilize a tribe of natives with a tribe of Kiwai and Mambare police boys, people who a couple of years ago were howling cannibals themselves.

But Frank was more conciliatory when he heard a false rumour that the Royal Commission of 1906 had recommended the dismissal of all Papuan police. The 'native police boy', he admitted, 'is one of my pet antipathies, but still the work he has to do might come in a bit awkward for a white man'.[27]

On his return from Keveri in 1906 Frank bought a cutter in Samarai. After returning the labourers to their home villages he 'spelled' in Samarai, recruited a new team and left for Tamata[28] By September he was established on Waterfall Creek, a tributary of the Gira. The shift back to the Gira may have been caused by gold becoming harder to find at Keveri but Frank had heard that Matt Crowe and Arthur Darling had gone prospecting up the Waria and he probably wanted to be at hand if the rush developed. Expenses at Waterfall Creek were high. An area first worked by miners about six years before, it was six days packing from Tamata's ill-supplied store. No food could be obtained by trade as the local villagers had left the area following trouble between themselves and the miners.[29]

When he shifted from Keveri to the Gira and the Waria in 1906 Frank became more involved in the events exciting the conversation and the politics of the miners. In 1905 Joe O'Brien was arrested and sentenced to two months' hard labour for assault. Charges that O'Brien had committed rape, murder and arson in the villages and had robbed Whittens were to be heard at the next sitting of the Central Court. Before any further hearings were held O'Brien smashed the skull of his guard, a member of the armed native constabulary, with an axe and escaped. Henry Griffin, the Assistant Resident Magistrate at Kokoda, instructed the Orokaiva people that if O'Brien shot at them they could spear him and he told the miners they were 'perfectly justified' in shooting him if he refused to surrender. The miners were divided by the case. Some believed that under no circumstances should any white man be made to work under a black guard: it would, said Staniforth Smith, then a Senator for Western Australia (later second-in-command to Sir Hubert Murray), 'revolutionize the views of natives in regard to the power and prestige of the white man [and make him] an object of contempt rather than of respect . . . as he should be'.[30] Some miners also strongly opposed the practice of Europeans being convicted on evidence given by Papuans, but seventeen Northern Division miners, including

Billy Little and Matt Crowe, signed a letter saying they did not condone the actions of 'escaped prisoner O'Brien'. When Frank Pryke reached the Northern Division he found that Little was intensely disliked for taking a lead in defending the actions of the officials but, he wrote to Dan on 8 December 1906, his own views were close to Little's:

O'Brien left himself open for it and in fact had been looking for it for some time previous to the affair and I don't think that I could manage to bring myself to sympathize very much with a man of the O'Brien stamp under any circumstances.

Little was also in disfavour over his nomination to the Legislative Council created by the Papua Act of 1905. At miners' meetings William Whitten had been chosen but, before the results of the meetings were known in Port Moresby, Little was appointed. Pryke believed that both Little and C. A. W. Monckton (who had first suggested Little's name to Acting Administrator F. R. Barton and then held ballots) had acted in good faith; Monckton did not know his earlier casual proposal had been accepted. While believing that one nominated miner would have slight influence on the government, Pryke thought Little might 'make a better member than any of the crowd who are doing most of the snorting'.[31]

Most of the miners were given the opportunity to express their grievances before the Royal Commission of 1906. The secretary of the Commission wrote to Pryke inviting him to give evidence and the letter was forwarded to Monckton at Kokoda who sent it on to Tamata. It reached Pryke at Waterfall Creek on 11 October, the same day the Commissioners heard evidence at Mambare beach. Waterfall Creek, a tributary of the Gira, was several days' walk and boat trip away from the beach, but that was the closest the Commissioners were coming. Pryke thought it was somehow typical of New

Guinea affairs.[32]

Frank worked at Waterfall for a few months only, then he and Jim, who had been ill with malaria, took the long trek across to the Waria where Matt Crowe and Arthur Darling had found gold. Ten days out from Tamata they reached the Waria where earlier arrivals told them it was a duffer. The Prykes went upstream and found a little gold on the Ono but it was very light and most of it went straight through the box. Coming back down-stream they located richer deposits which they worked till July 1907. Frank thought that Fred Kruger had done best of those who had gone to the Waria, but When the Prykes left the Waria for the first time in July 1907 they had 300 ounces, more than enough to pay their expenses and give them a spell in Australia.

The other event of the moment was the question of who would become the head of the administration of the area which in September 1906 had become the Australian Territory of Papua. Pryke thought the appointment of Staniforth Smith would be popular 'with the crowd', a few wanted the return of MacGregor but the retention of Barton would be most unpopular. Barton, said Frank, was 'unanimously and enthusiastically disliked.'[33] However, he was unable to find out why the dislike was so general nor could he discover any particular reason for it. Personally he did not think it mattered a great deal who was given the position. Apparently he did not consider the chief judicial officer, Hubert Murray, a candidate.

Back in Samarai from Cooktown in 1908 Pryke took a cutter he had bought in 1906 for two months' recruiting through the old ground around the islands and Milne Bay. While ashore he tried a dish in likely creeks and had a look at what was supposed to be a sheelite prospect on Fergusson Island. In March

Frank and Jim took the cutter into German New Guinea to enter the Waria River. When the miners had first crossed overland to the headwaters of the Waria they believed that they were liable to be penalised by German officials. Their entry into German territory was certainly illegal, but in 1908 Dr Albert Hahl, on a visit to the Waria, told the miners that they could take their stores up the river in order to mine in either Australian or German territory. Hahl's advice made access to the Waria field easier and ended the fears of those miners who were already working inside the German border.[34]

Realising the importance of the local people as a source of food and labour, Frank had cultivated the friendship of the villagers during his first year on the Waria. But in their second year the Prykes were involved in at least two bloody encounters. In October 1908 one of Edward Driscoll's labourers was killed by people from Wakaia.[35]

Driscoll, Frank, Jim, twenty-one Milne Bay labourers and fifteen Waria men from other areas, immediately set out for Wakaia. In his diary of the next few days Frank is more laconic than usual. Although the aim of the expedition was to punish there is no indication of what happened. But their employment of Waria men on the trip was significant. It was possible for miners to employ and trade with some peoples while fighting others. In fact, in some places it was difficult to maintain friendly relations with all groups. When miners participated in local conflicts they changed old balances of power and, free of concern about compensation payments or the need for future alliances, may have increased the degree of violence.

If Frank was restrained in his diary, he wrote without reserve to Dan on 9 February 1909 of another incident. After one of Darling's labourers was speared, then axed to death when he left the camp to get water, Frank and Darling immediately assumed it was their task to punish:

It was too late that night to do anything, but next morning Darling and I were among them just at daylight and gave them a bit of a shock, but I think by the way they got to cover they are used to being surprised or else they train for it, something like (alarm and rush) in fire practice. Anyhow they suffered heavily in pigs and would also have to build fresh houses. . . . They are a rather unsociable lot and are armed with the bow and arrow or skewer as Darling calls it. The weapons are much better than the spear as a native can send them over a hundred yards on level ground, and in that open grass country they must be able to send them long distances down the sides of the steep hills. Of course there was no chance of the nigs making a stand against us in a fair go as we were well armed, I had a Lee Enfield, Automatic Winchester, and two ordinary Winchesters and a shot gun and Darling was even better fitted out, but there are places about there where a large rock rolled with a bit of judgement, could wipe out an army.

In the same letter Frank noted that Murray had decided not to proceed against Charlie Ericksen and Joe Sloane, two miners charged with shooting a man on the Aikora.[36]

When Frank and Jim left the Waria in 1909 they were uncertain where they would go. The bird of paradise feathers they had sent to Tamata had been thrown away by the storekeeper worried by the government's arrest of other offenders; but they had enough gold to keep their 'noses in front of Bill Whitten's books'.[37] As for the Waria, Frank thought 'she [was] done'. Les Joubert, prospector and Buna storekeeper, suggested that they take his launch and try the rivers in German New Guinea. Although prepared to 'turn squarehead' Frank thought they might go back to Keveri if nothing came of the proposal to send a government prospecting expedition into new country.

Hoping to find a new field to support the one hundred alluvial miners then struggling to make a living in the Territory, the Papuan government in 1909 had agreed to pay £800 to meet the costs of a prospecting expedition. In a ballot to elect a leader the Waria and Gira miners voted for Frank Pryke and the Yodda for Matt Crowe.

Frank believed that had the Woodlark miners been given a vote he would have won.[38] When they met in Samarai Matt suggested that they toss for it, but eventually the composition of the party was resolved: Matt with the greater number of votes became the nominal leader and he selected Frank and Jim to accompany him.

Matt Crowe was about forty-seven years old, his thin frame could be straightened to 6ft 4in, and his tongue was caustic. Few miners and government officials had escaped Old Matt's 'keen sarcastic wit',[39] but all respected his skills as a prospector and bushman.

He had first met Frank and Dan in Western Australia, tried the Klondike gold fields in Canada, and had gone back to British New Guinea, where he had opened the Yodda in 1899. Frank was then thirty-seven, strongly built and just above medium height. He was no longer the young man who ran at athletic meetings, competed in fire brigade demonstrations, and played rugby as one of Baxter's boys in Goulburn; but he was tough and tireless in the bush, genial and patient as a companion. With thirty-five labourers and stores for three months the Prykes and Crowe left Port Moresby in June 1909 on the Merrie England.

From a base on the Tauri River they prospected the northern head-waters and then went east to the upper Lakekamu. In September they made canoes, went down the Lakekamu, met Hubert Murray, replenished their stores and returned up the

Frank Pryke's gold stamping batteries at Samarai, with a detail of his workers.

Lakekamu where they had found indications of gold. By foot, raft and canoe the expedition tested the gullies from the Tiveri to near Mt Lawson. On Ironstone Creek, a tributary of the Tiveri, they found good prospects and when they put in a box it returned two ounces a day.[40]

Small sturdy men wearing bark capes and armed with bows contested the right of the expedition to move through the area. They were Kapau speakers, the most south-eastern group of the Anga peoples: to the miners and government officials they were the Kukukukus. There were not many of them, wrote Frank, but they were tough and showered the prospectors with arrows every time they approached a village. The Prykes' head labourer, Waga Waga Dick, was killed instantly by an arrow through the heart. 'They set us again next morning', said Frank, 'but we had the best of that argument as we had got up before daylight and had gone to meet them'. In a cryptic reference to the same encounter Jim, in an undated letter from Ironstone Creek, recalled his days as a footballer: 'we ran into a couple of them coming down to have another pot at us, and the Goulburn scrum always was solid'. But the Kukukukus were not intimidated; they rejected all attempts to communicate with them and continued to 'salute' the camp with an occasional flight of 'skewers'.[41] For the life of the gold field relations between miners and villagers did not improve.

The Kukukukus would sometimes exchange food for steel axes and plane blades, but generally they avoided the intruders. Even where miners worked within half a day's walk of a village they rarely saw the inhabitants. A few iso-lated miners' camps and the government store were looted, some labourers who wandered into the bush were killed, and arrows were fired at prospectors. The violence was much less than it had been at Keveri or in the

Northern Division, but because of the reputation of the Kukukuku as fearless and unpredictable warriors and their rejection of attempts by gov-ernment officers and miners to change their way of life, the Kukukukus fascinated and disturbed the miners and their labourers. The Kukukuku on a peaceful mission was more likely to be shot at or have the dogs set on him than any other Papua New Guinean.

By the middle of December 1909 the prospectors were back in Port Moresby where they applied for a reward claim equal in area to forty men's claims. By confidential despatch and coded telegram from Thursday Island, Murray advised the Minister to caution impetuous Australians against joining the rush. Miners abandoned the Gira and the Yodda to try the new field; the stores at Tamata and Buna closed. Murray appointed three field officers to open a station at Nepa overlooking Ironstone Creek and he asked Dr Colin Simson to take a tem-porary position as government medical officer on the field. Frank and Jim Pryke recruited labourers in the southeast and were back on the Lakekamu by the end of January. While Jim and Matt worked the reward claim Frank prospected neigh-bouring gullies, hoping to pick up a rich patch, but the best returns came from the reward claim where they recovered up to five ounces a day.

In spite of attempts by Frank Pryke and the government to warn miners that the field was of limited extent, the find was 'boomed'.[42]

By the end of June over 1100 labourers and 200 white miners had gone to the field; 677 labourers and sixty-one miners were still there.[43] About 120 men crossed from Australia to Papua, but some did not reach the Tiveri and many of those who did had no labourers and no stores. The government repatri-

Port Moresby 1900 (top); Jim Pryke's reward claim mine 1910.

ated the destitute.

After six months the miners had recovered a total of about 3000 ounces of gold. The labourers were less fortunate: 258 of them were dead, most from dysentery. Over 400 had been admitted to the government's special dysentery hospital and 160 died there; the rest had died in the camps. Murray closed the field to further recruiting and while he was on leave Staniforth Smith considered moving all labourers to hospitals or quarantine areas away from the goldfield.[44]

The field was 'a little hell', said Frank Pryke. Seven of Crowe's and the Prykes' forty-one labourers died. Frank wrote to Dan:[45]

Living here is very expensive as you have to buy a lot of medicines and luxuries for the nigs to keep them alive at all and then you cannot get much work out of them as it is not safe to drive them and I tell you it grieves a man to lose one of them especially if he is a good boy. I have several of our old boys here. Bese and Gelua amongst them. I had a big contest to save Gelua as he was laid up for a month . . .

Frank was bitter about the death rate at the hospital and he told one story of a labourer asking his employer to hit him on the head with a tomahawk rather than send him to that place of death.

Frank thought that Simson's replacement, Dr Julius Streeter, having lost 200 cases in less than six months, 'must have put up a record'.[46] After the dysentery epidemic declined the labourers began to suffer from beriberi, a disease caused by a dietary deficiency; but with neither dysentery nor beriberi did the medical officers have the means or the knowledge to do much to arrest the debilitation and death of many men. In 1910-11 fifty-seven labourers died and in 1911-12 twenty-six died.

After travelling by foot, launch and government whaleboat Frank Pryke arrived in Port Moresby at the end of 1910 where he dined with Murray at Government House.[47] The Prykes had 'done fairly well' out of the reward claim although they had been paying £100 a month to the Tiveri store.[48] In Samarai the Lakekamu miners paid £1000 to their time-expired labourers and then led by the Prykes and Bob Bunting 'enlivened the town and danced the light fantastic'.[49] Recruiting for the return to the Lakekamu was difficult because of the many death notices which had been sent to Samarai the previous year. Patrol officers attempting to pay wages due to the relatives of dead men were besieged by villagers worried about men who had left as labourers, but by April Frank and Dan were back at the mouth of the Lakekamu with thirty-six recruits waiting for the Bulldog to take them upstream.[50] They had contracted to pay the men fifteen shillings a month, the same amount as they had paid the previous year.

During its second year the Lakekamu supported a population of about forty miners and 400 labourers spread from Cassowary Creek in the east to Olipai and Fish Creek thirty miles to the west.

The centre of the field was Whittens' store at Tiveri landing. There, one day's walk from Ironstone Creek, Frank Pryke heard the local news, did a bit of 'jubilating' and bought the butcher's bacon, dried apricots, dynamite, Winchester cartridges, pick handles, Dewar's whisky, quinine, Irish Moss Gum Jubes, rice, salmon, turkey red, dripping, rolled oats, golden syrup, flour, tin openers and Nestles milk which the labourers carried back to camp. When Frank sent a labourer down with a note to collect supplies Arthur Lumley attached the 'news' to the account: he listed who was in Tiveri 'on the shicker', invited Frank to come in and 'blow the froth off one' or listen to 'Melba at her best on the Phony graph', and added such important information as that the government medical officer had been drunk and 'tried to do it to Kruger's gin'. When the Bulldog failed to arrive and there was neither food nor news at the store Frank took a group of labourers out to make sago. The Prykes could have their own entertainment at Ironstone Creek with Jim's gramophone, although a musical evening could be disturbed by goats copulating under the floorboards. For 'literature' they had, Frank wrote to Dan on 2 September 1910, 'the [North Queensland Register] and the Bulletin with an occasional Novel or Magazine'.

In September 1911 the miners elected Frank Pryke to lead a prospecting expedition to be financed equally by miners and the government.[51] Pryke selected Robert Elliott and Charlie Priddle to go with him. In December the prospectors and forty-one labourers established a base 120 miles up the Vailala. Finding that the Iova, a turbulent north-western tributary flowing through narrow gorges, was impossible to prospect Pryke, Priddle and thirty carriers turned east and crossed a series of gullies where they found fine 'colours'. Although they saw gardens they met no people until 20 December when, at a point Frank thought was close to the German New Guinea border, they came to a village of twenty or thirty houses. The people accepted tobacco and appeared friendly, but as Pryke led the party on a track away from the village he was suddenly confronted by five or six men standing on a rock. He walked forward making signs to them to put their bows down; but one man released an arrow. Pryke shot and killed his attacker and the prospecting party 'shook tribe up generally'. The arrow had entered Pryke's chest 'just below left nipple and travelled down towards left kidney'. Frank pulled the arrow out then became 'pretty ill'.[52] Fearing he might die he dictated

The Prospectors of Sud-Est Goldfields (top); and Hydraulic
Sluicing in Papua (both by Charles Kerry 1913).

a note to Priddle describing what had happened and largely absolving the villagers from blame.[53] After camping for two days the party started back for the base camp carrying Pryke on a stretcher. The return journey took nine days. While Pryke recovered Priddle and Elliott tested the Ivori, another branch of the Vailala. By their return Pryke had recovered sufficiently to accompany Priddle up the Lohiki then south across country to the government station at Kerema. Frank Pryke's recovery was only slightly less dramatic than that described by Murray in his Annual Report:

Pryke is a man of iron nerve. An arrow went nearly through his body, and would probably have killed any one else; Mr Pryke, however, simply pulled it out and went on with his prospecting. [54] While waiting for a boat back to the Lakekamu the prospectors tried the Murua, but found only 'colours'. In March the Lakekamu miners learnt that the expedition had opened no new field. In spite of a second clash with villagers on the Lohiki and much tough travelling, all the carriers completed the return passage on the Bulldog.

Soon after the Vailala trip Frank and Jim left Papua to invest their Lakekamu gold in New South Wales. Frank purchased a share in a business in Moree. At the 'old curiousity shop' customers could buy tobacco, fancy goods, stationery, toys and newspapers, have a haircut or a game of billiards. But there were not many people in Moree in urgent need of these things and Frank soon decided that 'selling penny and half penny articles seems to be a mighty slow way of accumulating a fortune'. Worse still, he learnt that his partner, given to ill-founded optimism, was 'as mad as a dingo'.[55]

While wondering how to escape from Moree while he still had a little capital left, Frank was receiving letters about what was happening in Papua in letters from Priddle, Lumley, Bunting, Jourbet and Whitten. Newcombe had led a prospecting party across the head of the Oliipai and the Tauri; Matt Crowe, J. Preston, W. (Sharkeye) Park, and E. Auerbach had tried the Markham Valley in German New Guinea; and there was that Sir Rupert Clarke who owned hemp and coconut plantations in Papua was prepared to finance an expedition up the Fly. Jim too was 'talking Papua' when the Prykes were given the chance to return as members of Sir Rupert Clarke's expedition up the Fly.[56]

In January 1914 Frank Pryke celebrated the end of his career as a country businessman by going to two race meetings and a fight in Sydney before boarding the Matunga for Papua. In Port Moresby, Crowe, Priddle and 'other old acquaintances' assisted in the celebration of his arrival, then all attended a wedding where Frank 'got tight' and recited the 'Gippsland Girl'.[57] Six days later Frank was best man at Priddle's wedding. After his ageing liver had recovered Frank visited Archie MacAlpine, the manager of Clarke's plantation as Kanosia, and spent a week examining the country at the back of Galley Reach. Not finding anything of interest he sailed to Samarai, enlisted the assistance of ex-labourers, and recruited for the Fly trip. In Daru Frank and nineteen labourers joined the other members of the expedition, Clarke, MacAlpine, Jim and MacKay, an engineer. After a month exploring near the head of the Black and Palmer rivers, Clarke and MacAlpine returned to Daru, leaving MacKay and the Prykes with the launch Kismet to continue prospecting. For a further two months the Prykes dragged canoes and scrambled up the steep valleys of the Tully and Alice (Ok-Tedi). They had gone further up the Fly than any government expedition, and although they saw some 'likely looking country' and washed a few 'colours', they found nothing worth working.

Pryke's photograph from the Kismet expedition,
showing the Kukukus, and FP Chisholm compiling a
word dictionary with two elders.

On the Alice the Prykes had faced a crowd of about two hundred people who had attempted to persuade them to turn back. Many of the carriers thought this wise advice and Frank accepted that on a wage of one pound a month no man could be expected to take risks. By showing an apparent indifference to threats, the expedition passed without using force. In other areas the Prykes saw few people and they regretted the limited opportunities to trade.

Frank collected a fifty word vocabulary of the people of the 'Tully, Fly and Upper Alice Watersheds'[58] to add to the word-lists he had compiled for various other parts of Papua.

As the Prykes came downstream in September they met an apparently friendly group of about 100 men and women just below D'Albertis's Attack Point. After 'a good deal of trading' the river people invited those on the Kismet to come ashore and have a smoke. When the Prykes declined they were offered women, the women themselves beckoning and making 'immodest gestures and signs'. Just as the Prykes decided it would be prudent to move the Kismet into deeper water an old woman threw a burning stick onto the awning. More fire sticks and a flight of arrows followed. Those on the Kismet opened fire driving the attackers off. When calm was restored, five of the Prykes' labourers were wounded, Frank had an arrow through his forearm and Jim had a scratch on his stomach. On shore they found one man dead and they destroyed canoes and houses and cut down coconut trees. The Fly River warriors 'lined up as if they were going to give us battle, but unfortunately they thought better of it and bolted before we could get one'.[59] All the expedition members recovered quickly except Frank, who suffered intense pain and 'did some pretty rough penance' until his arm was attended by the Reverend Baxter Riley from the London Mission Society

Sir Rupert Clarke's *hosp'* up the Fly River.
The tribe who wore only a shell.
Frank Pryke on right. Frank is a very
immaculate individual when in civilization.

*Photograph of Frank Pryke on the Kismet Expedition
by Howard Dexter, 1914, courtesy of PAMBU.*

station in Daru.[60]

In November 1914 the Prykes returned to the Lakekamu, a field still supporting over twenty miners and 300 labourers. From a camp near Twisty Creek to the west of the Tiveri store they tested a few creeks, but getting only 'flyshits' they shifted back to work a claim not far from Ironstone Creek.[61] During the early months of 1915 they were more than covering their expenses, but either because the gold was worked out or because he was in need of medical treatment Frank left to try again to earn his living as a businessman. In August 1915 he became the proprietor of a billiard saloon in Burwood, Sydney. Dan, at various times newsagent, manager of a laundry, manufacturer of confectionery and owner of a hardware store, was also struggling to make a living in Sydney.

Jim went down from the Lakekamu with F. G. Chisholm, the patrol officer from Nepa, enlisted in the A.I.F., and after training in the snow and mud of Salisbury was killed at Broodseinde in 1917. Chisholm had been killed in France two weeks earlier.

Private James Alexander Pryke was forty-four when he died. In a tribute to 'a mate and brother' written nearly twenty years later Frank said that he too would have gone to the war but at the time Jim enlisted he had entered hospital 'to face the surgeon's knife'.[62]

From the early days of the Lakekamu field there had been attempts to promote dredging. In 1919 Frank Pryke took the Bulldog up the Lakekamu for the last time to re-examine some dredging leases.

The store, serving only six miners and their teams, was still at the landing; one government officer was at Nepa, but as he had received no supplies of rice or peas for over seven months

*Pryke's photographs show gold miners at
Lakekamu, and their workers.*

he was unable to go on patrol. Pryke's interest in dredging came to nothing, although following the development of Bulolo the Tiveri Gold Dredging Company was able to raise the capital to operate a small dredge on the Lakekamu from 1934 to 1939.

When Frank Pryke left Papua in 1919 the era of the independent alluvial miner had ended. The miners were no longer the most important export earners, the planters employed far more labourers, and Samarai and Port Moresby no longer boomed and slumped as the miners bought up stores to try a new field or paid off after twelve months on good dirt.

Trooper A.C. Lumley, one-time Whitten's Lakekamu storeman, wrote to Frank from the Australian Light Horse camp at Jericho that without a fresh strike Papua would be 'losing her best class of population.'[63] Aware of the inability of many miners to avoid trouble whether in town, village or bush, Frank Pryke also admired the diggers. Easily mistaken for unskilled labourers they were proud of their knowledge of bushmanship and mining. Without the power or resources of the government, they crossed hundreds of miles of unmapped country; and they were conscious that they were the agents of a new way of life for the peoples they encountered and the peoples they employed. They were competitive, irascible and generous. When Billy Ivory was ill during the first year at Lakekamu, the miners collected '160 quid' so that he could leave the field, but Frank was unsure whether they could persuade him to take it. [64] While Murray was hearing cases on the Mambare in 1905 he recorded one miner's complaint, 'Someone has been bandicooting my spuds.'[65] Some miners were uneducated, but Dan Horan was a journalist and Bob Newcombe a Bachelor of Science, and others read widely and were gifted conversationalists. The young Englishmen, Bishop Montague Stone-Wigg, enjoyed talking into the night with the miners when he stayed in their camps on the Yodda and Gira.[66] It was an awareness of these qualities and skills of the miners, as well as a sense of camaraderie, which led Frank Pryke to write that 'the miners were the best class of people to open up new country.' [67]

The miners had certainly opened up new country. They were more numerous, more inclined to go inland, and employed more people than any other group in British New Guinea. They formed closer relationships with the people than did the white missionaries or government officials. But they may not have been the 'best class' to be the carriers of a cultural revolution.[68] The miners, in changing relations between groups, increasing movement, and modifying the economy by introducing new materials, new crops and greatly reducing the numbers of birds, fish and animals in the area, may have intensified the warfare among the Keveri. But there was one important restraining and humanising influence on the miners; they needed New Guineans.

Generally European miners did not travel or work claims in New Guinea without New Guinean labourers. Several who tried to do so died. In the main recruiting grounds of the south-east the labourers made their choice freely and knowingly. When Frank Pryke went ashore at Wadelei village on Fergusson Island in 1908 and found some of his old labourers, they told him they had just been working in Woodlark and were not interested in recruiting. Pryke could only move on. By 1908 many men had recruited several times and the area had been recruited long enough for some labourers to be the sons of earlier recruits. They knew the skills of the alluvial miners and a few had become independent miners working gold on old fields in the islands. Frank normally left a group working a box while he prospected neighbouring country. Often he sent the labourers to nearby villages to trade for food. Other miners equipped labourers with a pick and pan and sent them out to look for new ground. In fact 'Most of the prospecting on the Waria appeared to be done by boys'.[69] The independent movement of labourers meant that the white miners sometimes had no influence on and no knowledge of encounters between labourers and villagers.

On the Gira, Yodda, Keveri, Waria and Lakekamu the miners armed some of their labourers. The handing of the gun to the labourer demonstrated the interdependence of miner and labourer in the bush, and in that act the miner gave up much of his advantage in power over the labourer. In fact after 1900 a miner was as likely to be killed by his own labourers as he was by hostile villagers. In the field it was in the interests of the miners to maintain friendly relations with local peoples: they needed them as guides, carriers and suppliers of food. Without the numerous peoples and gardens on the upper Waria it would have been impossible for the miners to have worked an area so far from a store.

While critical of any government official or miner who needlessly disturbed relations with local villagers most miners believed it was necessary to use a ruthless punitive raid when a carrier or miner was killed. On the Mambare, Gira and the Waria some raids drove people from their home areas and ended their relations with the miners. On the Lakekamu, where the Anga were hostile to foreigners and had little desire to trade with the miners and the miners did not need them, one side normally avoided the other, and when they did meet there was violence.

On his return to Australia in 1919 Pryke leased a hotel in Maryborough, Queensland, but the working men of the area failed to drink as much as he expected. Back in Sydney he 'had more luck with his business speculations'.[70] In 1925 when he married Ina Cruickshank, a thirty-nine year old divorcee, he described himself as a storekeeper.[71] and they moved into the rooms above his store in Rushcutters Bay. But running a suburban business was not Frank Pryke's first choice of occupation. From letters, newspapers and the talk in Usher's Bar he kept informed about events in New Guinea. By 1925 the talk was that 'on the Bulolo old Sharkeye's getting gold'.[72]

By 1915 the south-east of Papua had been prospected intensively and most of the southward flowing rivers had been tested. In the north the miners had been up the Kumusi, Mambare, Gira and Waria. Obviously the next step was to try those rivers taking their rise not far from the headwaters of the Lakekamu and the Waria: the Bulolo and the Watut. When Sharkeye Park and Jack Nettleton began working gold on Koranga Creek in 1922 old miners disputed whether they were on new ground or whether they had relocated strikes made earlier by either A. Darling or J. Preston; but by the end of 1922 both 'Buna" Darling and Jimmy Preston were dead.[73]. At first there was no rush to Koranga. Park and Nettleton said little, the field was difficult to reach, the people of the area were known to be hostile, and the cost of stores landed at Salamaua and carried to the field were so high that only those on rich ground could afford to stay there. In January 1926 William Royal and one labourer climbed a series of rock faces to reach a spur above the point where the upper Edie cascades into the lower Edie. Finding good prospects, he returned to test the area more thoroughly and washed up to seven pennyweights in a dish. Royal's worries about feeding his labourers and paying off his £700 debt to Burns Philp were almost over.[74]

Royal, who had been on the Western Australian goldfields in 'the early days', was known as an optimist and some men

Frank Pryke's camp at Edie Creek 1927 (top); and his view of a miner's camp at the junction of th Edie and Merri Creeks, "one of the picked spots." 1928

waited for confirmation of the Edie Creek find, but Frank Pryke, knowing the importance of being early to a new strike and realising this was probably his last chance to be there when they found the big one, was among the first of those who arrived from Australia.[75] By May he had recruited labourers and made the walk up the Gadugadu track from Salamaua to Edie. It was, he said, 'the worst road I had ever seen food packed over to a goldfield'. Edie, at an altitude of over 6000 feet, was 'very cold and wet — a miserable kind of place'.[76] Les Joubert, delayed when his carriers deserted, arrived to work in partnership with Pryke. In September the main rush began and by November there were 219 miners and 1324 indentured labourers on the field.

At first handicapped by the confusion over whether New Guinea mining laws permitted men intending to work with box and pan to take up large dredging and sluicing leases, Pryke and Joubert eventually worked several small claims on the Merri, a tributary of the Edie. For Pryke the events of 1926 followed a familiar pattern. The villagers raided the carriers on the track from Salamaua and government officials, miners and labourers combined in punitive expeditions. In September dysentery broke out at Salamaua. While the death rate was much less than at the Lakekamu forty-eight men had died of the disease by early 1927.[77] Four of Pryke's thirty-one labourers died, two at Salamaua, one on the track and one at Edie.

But there were differences. Firstly Frank was fifty-four years old: he found Komiatum hill a tough climb and he knew that twenty years earlier he would have made the crest with ease. Less able to prospect new areas, he made only one trip from the main field; in June he went back to old ground in the hope that beaches on the Waria would be worth taking up as

Frank Pryke and Les Joubert's first camp at Koranga Creek.

dredging leases. At the end of the year he had lost three stone in weight and he spent some time in the Rabaul hospital.[78] In his 1928 diary he recorded a lament for his passing vigour:

My roving days are over,
My naughty nights are out,
What was once my sex appeal,
Is now a water spout.

Secondly he had to recruit his labourers in New Guinea and he had to speak to them in the Pidgin of the New Guinea employers.

Thirdly there was more gold than the old Papuan prospectors had ever seen. From one claim 100 feet by 200 feet Pryke and Joubert obtained over 2000 ounces.[79] Where a good strike in Papua had supported two or three stores, the Morobe gold fields stimulated the growth of towns at Salamaua, Wau and Lae. After the first year on the Lakekamu Jack Murphy's fifty pound shout at Tommy McCrann's in Port Moresby became a legend; at Salamaua the champagne shouts were frequent. At the end of 1929 the manager of the Bank of New South Wales recorded that the 'record single shout' resulted in the consumption of eighty-four bottles purchased at thirty shillings each. The corks had been nailed to the ceiling as evidence. Few of the 'old crowd' were there to see the new wealth.

Many of those who had followed the strikes from Woodlark to the Gira, Yodda, Milne Bay, Aikora, Keveri, Waria and Lakekamu were dead. Matt Crowe, perhaps the best known of the pioneer prospectors, died in Samarai just six months before Royal washed gold at Edie. Frank thought only one in ten of those on the Morobe gold field in 1927 could be classed as experienced miners.

When Pryke returned to the gold field in 1928 there were

further changes. He flew from Lae to Wau by Junkers in 35 minutes; and in July his wife 'with about half ton of impedimenta' arrived for a three month stay. But there were still picks to sharpen, gardens to plant for fresh food, floods that swept down breaking dams and carrying away flumes, and miners who dropped in for a yarn. The gold yield remained high; when they weighed up on Fridays they recorded totals of up to 100 ounces of fine gold and specimens.[80]

On all the Papuan fields the alluvial miners had dreamed of promoting a big dredging company or finding the mother lode.

Dredges and reefs were worked in Papua but generally long after those who had opened the field had left. On the Morobe gold fields gold-bearing quartz veins were found on Edie in 1927 and even before Royal climbed to Upper Edie some men had realised the vast potential of the Bulolo Valley for dredging. Companies with a greater nominal capital than on any Australian gold field were formed to work reefs, sluice and dredge on the Morobe. Pryke and Joubert were able to sell 'one of the best private leases' to the Koranga Gold Sluicing Company.[81] Frank retired to live in Coogee, Sydney. One New Guinea gold field had fulfilled all the promises.

In retirement Frank Pryke was often ill with arthritis, hydatids and finally heart disease; but he kept travelling by car through the country around Bathurst and Goulburn which he had known as a young man, and by ship to the islands, Japan and England where he poked around Bury St Edmunds looking for traces of his father's family. In 1932 he went with Fred Kruger to have a look at a gold prospect in Milne Bay (and found the thirteen mile walk exhausted his sixteen stone body), considered pegging sulphur springs on Fergusson Island, and with the help of an old villager relocated a mica deposit he and Dan had found thirty years before. The waiting on beaches reminded him of former days when they complained that they spent half their lives waiting for boats. In many villages he met 'old boys'. Some brought gifts and Pryke realised they were making investments as well as giving presents for he was expected to give something in return. He was pleased to hear that one man, Lolo, had taken twenty ounces of gold into Samarai explaining that he had been able to find it because he had once worked for Frank Pryke. Having an affection for Samarai which he never felt for Port Moresby or Rabaul, Pryke was disappointed on his return to the island. Samarai was neater, it had electric light and an ice-works, but it had[82] *'grown quite slack and respectable and even the government officers seem[ed] to have reduced considerably their average daily consumption of booze. One missed the wild doings and boisterous nights when the miners from the Yodda and Ikora gambled, fought and drank . . .'*

One 'very old . . . acquaintance, malaria' affected him in exactly the same way as it had in the past.

Within a context which gave power and prestige to the employer and attempted to ensure only the survival of the labourer, Frank Pryke had shown concern for the welfare of his labourers. He rarely used 'physical argument' and he provided better conditions for his men than the minimum prescribed in the Native Labour Ordinance.

Having spent many months in the Milne Bay area, some-times sleeping in the villages, he knew the way of life of his labourers and he felt affection for some who went with him on several trips. He maintained a close relationship with peoples in the recruiting area for thirty years: when he saw some of his ex-labourers on his last voyage through the islands they were old men.

Curious about the peoples he met on prospecting trips, he made brief notes about their houses, weapons, gardens and physical appearance; and he collected vocabularies. In distinguishing groups by their reactions to the miners he was inclined to use simplistic generalisations: the Kukukuku were fearless and treacherous, the Keveri were friendly. By comparison other less perceptive and knowledgeable miners gathered all New Guineans under one sweeping condemnation. While he was aware that people seeing miners for the first time could not know whether they were weak or strong, friendly or hostile, he was critical of the missionaries who, he said, too frequently assumed that the New Guineans were blameless. Pryke argued that he had been in situations where he had had to shoot to survive, but that he had never killed wantonly.[83] While it was true that Pryke had avoided needless bloodshed, he had participated in punitive raids when the immediate risk to himself and others had passed. The punitive raid was carried out either for vengeance or to prevent further attacks and thereby reduce the total number of deaths: it was not an act of desperate self-preservation.

Against this it must be said that Pryke had also been in situations where he had endangered himself by showing extraordinary restraint. Hubert Murray who found little in most men to justify public praise said Pryke was 'known throughout the Territory for his kind and tactful treatment of natives'; he was of 'humane disposition'.[84]

Writing openly of most events in his letters and diaries, Pryke never mentioned his relations with Papuan women. Lumley, whose letters were neither inhibited nor serious, accused Frank of 'acolyting virgins up and down the coast', and in another letter he said that Jim should have married one of the Papuan women 'amongst whom he laboured so laboriously and so long'.[85] It is difficult to see a man of Pryke's temperament raising hell in all the villages along the coast, but on his leisurely trips around Milne Bay and the islands he he was probably not solely concerned with getting the team home and arranging for new recruits. Around 1910 Pryke seems to have formed a longer relationship with a Milne Bay woman, Dadawe, who bore him a son. When Dadawe died, the son, still an infant, was brought up as a member of another family resulting from inter-racial marriage. Many other miners and traders who lived in the southeast from the 1890s formed relationships of varying types and for varying lengths of time with women of the area.

In a note-book Pryke recorded what is probably part of a ship-board conversation:

'How long ago since you started writing poetry?
I started when I was 60 years old.

What a pity you did not start when you were young. You might have been a poet by now – what a peculiar combination, prospecting and poetry. [86]

His poems are about people and places near Bathurst and Goulburn in New South Wales and on the gold fields of Papua and New Guinea. The places are praised and Pryke is always generous to his fellow men; but the poems still express the frustrations of the wanderer, whose achievements have been in the bush, now old, ill, instructed in what he can eat and drink by doctors and bored at bridge parties attended to please a wife. Collected in a privately printed edition after Pryke's death, they are likely to be read only by those interested in the writer and his times. Most of the poems are slight, lack detail and the language is derivative: the ocean is blue, the palms tall, the breeze gentle and the morning bright and early. The rare arresting line occurs when Pryke adapts the language of the diggers to write of a personal experience; when he 'swamped it to Coolgardie' or 'fattened up the leeches Away along the Bida track'.[87] Diffident about displaying his verses, Pryke had no illusions about their merit: they were 'crude and halt and lame'.[88] Able to write a sharp and interesting letter, Frank Pryke made a mistake when he chose to put in verse his memories of football matches against the cockies of Collector, of old mining fields, mates, prospecting trips, and conflicts on the Vailala and the Fly.

During his first year on the Lakekamu Frank wrote to Dan that a priest from the Sacred Heart Mission on Yule Island had visited the field: 'He came and hunted me up but I was not taking any. Old Matt sooled him on to me'.[89] Instructed in Roman Catholicism as a child, Frank was married and cremated in ceremonies directed by Anglican clergymen. He had come to believe that no man could be certain what happened after death, and if men were to be judged in an after-life then the decision was not to be altered by performing ritual or 'putting shillings in the plate'.[90] When he was rich, sick and old, he frequently thought about men he had known, men who had battled on to die in old men's homes, who were killed in the war, who made fortunes and lost it in bookmakers' bags. A man, he concluded, could determine his fate to only 'a very limited extent'.[91] All men, constantly subjected to a variety of forces, were given some opportunities for self-advancement, and those with more ability, luck or determination used their chances. The good man was the trier who did not squeal in bad times nor get 'uppish' in good. He chose his friends carefully and never let a comrade down. He judged other men not by their nationality, or their breeding (some men of fine pedigree were hanged), or their talk, or their possessions, but by

(Top) Daniel Pryke with his wife Mary, and (from left) Dan, Mark and Frank in Armidale, 1914. (Bottom) Dan Pryke (right) with son Mark behind, in front of his ironmongery, Kensington 1920.

their actions.[92] The good times to be remembered were when pearlers, traders and miners met in a bar in Samarai, undivided by poverty or wealth or petty disputes; the money of six men on the bar ready to pay for the next round of drinks. The men to be admired were those who did not turn back at a shower of arrows or when the stores were short, they conquered their environment; in the past they had been sailors and bushmen, by the time Frank Pryke left New Guinea they were aviators. Other men followed and profited on their tracks. Frank Pryke hoped, but did not say, that he had gone a bit further and others had benefited.

Frank Pryke died at his home in Coogee 5 August 1937. His ashes were buried on the hill at Samarai. A plaque was placed on the wall of the War Memorial and Library Institute in memory of 'this British Gentleman', but a phrase he may have appreciated more appeared in an obituary: he possessed 'all the finest qualities of mateship'.[93]

Frank Pryke's name fitted easily into a traditional story told of old diggers. It was a story he himself had heard many times.[94] When Frank arrived at the gates of heaven Saint Peter asked him who he was.

'Frank Pryke, prospector' said Frank.

A look of despair came over Saint Peter:

'Not another one!'

Frank, who thought his old mates weren't a bad crowd, asked, 'What's the matter with prospectors?'

Saint Peter just opened the gate and pointed across a large valley leading to a distant mansion. Men were pegging dredging leases, alluvial rights, reefing prospects, homestead leases and water-rights; they were cutting races, erecting flumes, putting in boxes, ground sluicing, hydraulicking, clearing tail races, panning, pulling rocks out of the riffles and shovelling wash. The road had been dug up, trees felled and streams were dammed and dirty.

'No trouble to shift this crowd', said Frank, and walked over to the nearest man and said a few words. In a few minutes, Matt Crowe, Arthur Darling, Fat Priddle, Bob Newcombe, Billy Ivory, Billy Little, Tom the Jockey, Little George, Old Jew, Red Ned Parke, Andy Doyle, Lucky Joe Sloane, Sharkeye Parke, Peter Bourke and Fred Kruger had gone past and within a couple of hours the field was clear.

'What did you say to man?' asked Saint Peter.

Frank was packing rice in forty pound bundles and took a while to answer. 'I just said that I heard a bloke in a place below here had a full shammy. It was a bit hot, but he was cleaning up four ounces a day.' Frank Moved out the gate.

'Hey where are you going?' called Saint Peter.

'Well,' said Frank. 'there could be something in that story.'

Frank Pryke, trading in the Fly River, 1914.

BIBLIOGRAPHY

The main collection of Frank Pryke's extant writings is in the National Library of Australia, Canberra (N.L., MS. 1826), held in trust for the Papua New Guinea archives. This includes diaries for parts of most years between 1903 and 1915, a series of letters from Frank to Dan, 1905 to 1920, a few letters and two diaries by Jim, letters and notes by A. C. Lumley to Frank, labour contracts, accounts and bank books.

The Mitchell Library, Sydney (M.L., A 2616 and A 2617) has Frank's diaries for 1928, 1932, and part of another year, perhaps 1929, a diary of the Vailala trip 1911-12, a typed report by Frank on the Fly expedition of 1914 and a collection of newspaper cuttings most of which are not identified.

The cover and title page of Pryke's 286 page volume of poems merely say 'Poems Frank Pryke New Guinea': there is no introduction, no date of publication and no printer. The Mitchell Library catalogue suggests that an edition of only about fifty copies was published in 1944. Mr Frank Pryke of Sydney (a nephew) suggests that Ina Pryke had the poems printed in Hong Kong in 1937. Mr Frank Pryke and his daughter Mrs L. Christopherson answered many questions about the family and let me look at papers in their possession. These included Les Joubert's diary of 1927, an album of Frank's photographs, newspaper cuttings, notes on the Fly expedition and other papers. Mr Leo Pryke, another nephew now living in Sydney, also provided information.

The Papuan Times (from 1911) and its successor, the Papuan Courier, reported the movements of the miners and published reports by Frank on his prospecting trips. Frank gave evidence to the Royal Commission on the Edie Creek (New Guinea) Leases, 1927, and the transcript of the evidence is in the Commonwealth Archives Office (C.A.O., CP 660 Series 25, Vol. 1). Diaries by C. S. Robinson (National Archives of Papua New Guinea), Bishop Montague Stone-Wigg (Library, University of Papua and New Guinea), and J. H. P. Murray (Mitchell Library), have comments on the Papuan gold fields. J. H. W. Johns (Letters, University of Melbourne Archives) made detailed observations on the Morobe gold fields from 1929 to 1932.

In the Papua New Guinea National Archives are the patrol reports and station journals kept by government officers administering the gold fields. They are very full for Nepa from 1910 to 1920 because the government officers there were almost solely concerned with the administration of the Lakekamu gold field. The Annual Reports of British New Guinea, Papua, and Australian New Guinea reprint some Wardens' reports and provide other information.

Two detailed obituaries were published, by Fred Kruger in the Papuan Courier 22 October 1937 and by Mrs A. A. Innes in Pacific Islands Monthly, Vol. 6, No. 1, August 1937. Dr T. Dutton, Linguistics Dept., R.S.P.S., A.N.U. helped sort out the languages of those people living close to the gold fields. Jim Gibbney, Australian Dictionary of Biography, helped trace documentary material.

NOTES

1. Frank Pryke's parents were John Pryke, born in London c1829 and Catherine (nee McKelvey), born in Ireland c1835. John and Catherine were married in Beechworth, Victoria in 1860 and moved to Sofala where the Pryke brothers were born. Frank was their seventh child.

2. Notes in a small coverless book probably written about five years after the events they describe (N.L., MS. 1826). See also Report on Musa expedition, Sydney Mail, 1 May 1897, p. 955.

3. The death of Green is discussed by John Waiko in 'A Payback Murder: the Green bloodbath', Journal of the Papua and New Guinea Society, Vol. 4, No. 2, 1970, pp. 27-35.

4. All quotes in this section are from Frank's diary of the trip (N.L., MS. 1826). Written in a small notebook, it gives no year, but Finnigan's was found early in 1899. I have changed Pryke's spelling of some place names, e.g. Mambari to Mambare.

5. British New Guinea, Annual Report 1898-99, p. 90.

6. Presumably 'per man' means just Pryke and Klotz and does not include their ten labourers. The gold was worth about seven dollars an ounce.

7. 'Little George' eventually found gold on the Morobe gold field. By the time he died in 1939, he had spent forty-six years chasing gold in New Guinea.

8. The Keveri find is not described by either Dan or Frank. See Fred Kruger's obituary of Frank in the Papuan Courier, 22 October 1937. Kruger was a close friend of Pryke.

9. F. E. Williams, 'Mission Influence among the Keveri of South-East Papua', Oceania, Vol. 15, No. 2, 1944, pp. 90-1, has a map and description.

10. From Jim's diary for 1906, between pages 80 and 81 (N.L., MS. 1826). There are two other poems in the diary 'Kwato Speaks'; on the death of Robinson, and 'The Champagne's getting flat, Les.'

11. Many of these villages have shifted since the days of the miners.

12. Frank to Dan, 13 October 1905 (N.L., MS. 1826).

13. British New Guinea, Annual Report 1904-05, p. 23 says twenty-four miners were on the field and 1906-07, p. 8 says fifteen was the maximum.

14. Frank to Dan, 5 March 1906, and diary, 18 February 1906 (N.L., MS. 1826).

15. Frank to Dan, 6 August 1906.

16. Dan to 'Minnie' Steenson, 11 March 1905 (N.L., MS. 1826).

17. Both Dan and Frank's diaries of this incident have survived.

18. This section is based on Williams, 'Mission Influence' and T. Dutton, Languages of South-East Papua: a preliminary report (Canberra, 1971).

19. The patrol had been led by English, Blayney and Barton.

20. F.E. Williams, op. cit. 100

21. British New Guinea, Annual Report 1903-04, p. 26.

22. Frank to Dan, 13 October 1905.

23. Annual report, 1904-05, p23.

24. Frank to Dan, 13 July 1905.

25. Frank to Dan 13 July 1905. The case was noted in the Register of Criminal Cases, Central Court, British New Guinea, 20 May 1905.

26. Frank, diary, 2 April 1906 (ibid.).

27. Frank to Dan, 18 December 1906 (ibid.).

28. Frank to Dan, 6 August 1906.

29. Frank to Dan, 20 September 1906. A. Darling was born in Canada and grew up in Queensland. He died in 1911 aged about 40. Some people have said he might have made the first find on Koranga Creek

30. Frank, Diary, Mitchell Library. This is a small undated notebook. It includes a diary of a trip from Rabaul to Vila and Noumea.

31. Frank to Dan, 17 December 1909 (N.L., MS. 1826).

32. Frank to Dan, 8 December 1906 (N.L., MS. 1826).

33. Frank to Dan 8 December 1906.

34. A draft of a letter to the editor of the North Queensland Register is on the blotter pages of Frank's diary beginning opposite the entry for 27 August 1908 (N.L., MS. 1826). It sets out what Frank thought German policy was. The published letter is in the unidentified newspaper cuttings in the Mitchell Library. When the miners first crossed into German New Guinea they also violated the Native Labour Ordinance, which made it illegal to take labourers from British New Guinea. On Hahl see Chapter 2.

35. Frank's diary, 22 October 1908 (N.L., MS. 1826). Chinnery locates 'Wakai-ia' in the Morobe District between the Waria and the Papua-New Guinea border above the point where the Waria crosses the eighth parallel for the first time. Pryke traded with the Wakaia both before and after the punitive raid.

36. Frank to Dan, 9 February 1909. Frank calls the people Gaswak(?); he probably refers to the Guswei to the north-west of Garaina. Chinnery reported finding one seven and a half foot bow on the Waria. Murray says that when he arrived at the Aiko/a he was talking to Erichsen [s/c] who asked: ' "When do you expect the Yoodge?" I said, " I am the Judge" . He said " Oh Christ!" ' Murray also recorded that the miners wanted 'to deal it out' to the Wagaia, who lived in German New Guinea. The Wagaia was presumably Frank Pryke's Wakaia. J. H. P. Murray, diary, 29 December 1908, and 2 January 1909 (M.L.).

37. Frank to Dan, 9 February 1909 (N.L., MS. 1826). One man Murray decided to charge with the illegal shooting of birds was H. L. Griffin who immediately resigned from the government service.

38. Frank to Dan, 4 April 1909. See also Australian Archives, Papua, Mines Papers, 1907-27, G.70, Item 1907/87.

39. Frank, Poems, p. 46. The poem 'Matt Crowe' was also printed in Pacific Islands Monthly, Vol. 4, No. 11, June 1935, p. 6.

40. There is no diary of this trip, but it is described in letters by Jim and Frank (N.L., MS. 1826) and in Murray's despatches to the Minister, 24 September, 11 December 1909 (P.N.G. Archives).

41. 'Jim writes "skewers" to use diggerese' Jim to Dan, no date, written from Ironstone Creek, probably at the end of 1909.

42. Jim to Dan, 4 January 1910.

43. Papua, Annual Report 1909-10, pp. 124-5.

44. Smith to Minister, 4 and 21 July 1910 (P.N.G. Archives).

45. Frank to Dan, 20 May 1910 (N.L., MS. 1826). Gelua and Bete [s/c] both survived to be paid off in Samarai (labour contracts).

46. Frank to Dan, 2 September 1910.

47. Frank, diary, December 1910.

48. Frank to Dan, 2 September 1910. Just how well the Prykes did on the Lakekamu is not clear. By September of 1910 Frank thought they would 'clear a thou' each' for the first year. The reward claim yielded over 1400 ounces in the first twelve months (Warden's Report, P.N.G. Archives).

49. Frank, Poems, p. 46. The poem 'Matt Crowe' was also printed in Pacific Islands Monthly, Vol. 4, No. 11, June 1935, p. 6.

50. Frank to Dan, 14 April 1911 (N.L., MS. 1826).

51. Papuan Times, 20 March 1912. Account of Vailala trip by Pryke (rough notebook, N.L., MS. 1826). More carefully written diary in the Mitchell.

52. The quotes are from the notebook in the National Library.

53. 'Fat' Priddle may have been a fine prospector but he was a poor hand with the pencil. Priddle's writing is now difficult to read and his spelling was erratic.

54. Pacific Islands Monthly, Vol. 6, No. 1, August 1937, p. 74.

55. Frank to Dan, 28 July [1912?]; 19 August 1913 (N.L. MS. 1826).

56. Frank to Dan, 28 July (1912?); 19 August 1913 (N.L. MS. 1826).

57. Frank, diary, January 1914.

58. Frank's rough diary of the trip is in the National Library and there is a typed report, which includes the word-list, in the Mitchell. Among the newspaper cuttings in the Mitchell Library is an exchange of letters between Leo Austin and Frank Pryke about how far the Prykes went up the Fly. No dates are given but the letters are from the Sydney Morning Herald. Further information about the Fly expedition is contained in papers obtained from Mr F. Pryke of Sydney (a nephew of Frank) and now in the possession of his daughter,

Mrs Leonie Christopherson.

59. In the typed account Frank does not say they killed anyone. He did, however, report the killing to the government. Murray to Minister, 7 October 1914 (P.N.G. Archives) includes statement by Frank. The quote is from papers held by Mrs L. Christopherson.

60. One carrier, Miki, from Normanby Island, died on the trip. Other men said it was because magic had been made against him for not building a garden for his mother. Frank thought that if this was so it may have been a record for long distance pouri pouri.

61. Frank, diary (N.L., MS. 1826).

62. Frank, Poems, p. 25. 'To a Mate and Brother'. Frank had an operation for the removal of hydatids. Bill Gammage checked the records at the Australian War Memorial to obtain information about Jim Pryke.

63. Lumley to Frank, 6 April 1918.

64. Frank to Dan, 20 May 1910 (N.L., MS. 1826).

65. Murray, Diary, 15 May 1905.

66. M. Stone-Wigg, Diary example 30 June 1904.

67. He said that Hahl allowed the miners into German New Guinea because he knew they were 'the best class of people to open up new country'. Letter to editor of North Queensland Register, 1908.

68. Letter to editor, North Queensland Register, op.cit; see note 34).

69. Frank, diary, 24 June 1908 (N.L., MS. 1826).

70. Fred Kruger, obituary of Frank, Papuan Courier 22 October 1937.

71. On the marriage certificate, Ina Cruikshank was born

Howard in Orange.

72. Frank, Poems, 'Usher's Bar', p. 116; 'Bulolo Gold', p. 140. The latter appeared also in Pacific Islands Monthly, Vol. 4, No. 4, November 1934, p. 30.

73. Healey and others have accepted that Darling did find gold. E. Aurbach, Pacific Islands Monthly, July 1940, who went up the Markham with Matt Crowe and others in 1912, claimed that Darling did not find gold on the Koranga. Perhaps the best evidence is in Murray's diary (at least it establishes the date). He records on 28 December 1909 that Darling was back, had found gold, and was riddled with arrows. The obvious reason why no-one took much notice of Darling's find (if there was one) is that he reported it at the same time as Crowe and the Pryke's got back from Lakekamu.

74. Royal described his discovery in evidence before the Royal Commission 1927, transcript of evidence, pp. 1294-7 (C. A.O., CP. 660, Series 25, Vol. 1).

75. In 'Bulolo Gold' are the lines:

Though disillusion greeted us on many a previous trip

It may be our last and lucky chance, we must not let it slip.

76. Royal Commission 1927, transcript of evidence, Frank Pryke's evidence, p. 156; Joubert's evidence, pp. 887-93 (C.A.O., CD. 660, Series 25, Vol. 1).

77. Dr R. W. Cilento, Director of Public Health, argued at great length to show that all possible had been done to prevent the spread of disease on the Morobe gold field, and that there had been only 'trivial mortality'. Royal Commission 1927, transcript of evidence, p. 1102 (ibid).

78. Ibid., p. 116. Pryke said that all who had been on Edie suffered in health.

79. Ibid., p.892.

80. Frank, diary, 1928 (M.L., A 2616). Ina arrived 20 July

1928. In 1927 Leo Pryke, Frank's nephew, now living in Sydney, went to work for Frank at Koranga.

81. From an unidentified press cutting in the Pryke Papers (M.L.).

82. Frank, diary, 2 August 1932 (M.L., A 2617). All this paragraph is based on the 1932 diary. In earlier times Frank had been about twelve stone.

83. Two poems make interesting comments on violence between miners and villagers, 'Gone West' and 'The Yodda', Poems, pp. 49, 129.

84. Papua, Annual Report 1911-12. There is a chance that Murray was anticipating criticism about letting miners enter territory not controlled by the government.

85. Lumley to Frank, 21 June 1912 and 3 February 1913 (N.L., MS. 1826).

86. Frank, Diary, Mitchell Library. This is a small undated notebook. It includes a diary of a trip from Rabaul to Vila and Noumea.

87. Frank, Poems, 'The Gully Raking Days', p. 12 and 'To a Mate and Brother', p. 35. Bida (or Beda) is in the Chirima.

88. Ibid.,'The Goddess of Verse', p. 159.

89. Frank to Dan, 20 May 1910 (N.L. MS.1826).

90. Frank, Poems, 'The Cemetery', p. 30. Jim told the army he was a Roman Catholic.

91. Ibid .,'The Winds of Fate', p. 27.

92. I. L. Idriess, who consulted Frank Pryke, says Pryke was a 'level-headed man . . . who always treats the savage as a man like himself'. (Gold-Dust and Ashes, Sydney, first printed in 1933 and reprinted twenty-three times before it was issued as a paperback in 1964), p. 9

93. Pacific Islands Monthly, Vol. 6, No. 1, August 1937, p. 74.

94. Frank, Poems, 'The Rush', page 120, puts the story into verse.

Frank Pryke on his arrival in Sydney, 1936 as photographed by the Sydney Morning Herald *(NLA collection).*

A Woman Gold Seeker

Mrs Pryke of Koranga Creek, New Guinea

ION IDRIESS

Australian Woman's Mirror, August 1930

To the staunch hearted women who have braved the dangers of a savage land add Mrs Frank Pryke of Koranga Creek, New Guinea goldfields. Fate eventually smiled on Mrs Pryke, for she won through to gold and fortune—unlike the first white woman to reach Edie Creek, the luckless Mrs Muller, who climbed the dreadful Byang Wack. On Koranga Creek Mrs Muller's husband was killed by a falling tree soon afterwards, and eventually, after having braved so much, she walked out again a lonely and pathetic figure. Mrs Doris Booth, author of Mountains, Gold, and Cannibals, was the first white woman on Bulolo. She was also a lucky one who secured both fame and fortune. Mrs Prykes husband, a well known prospector who has located four New Guinea goldfields, and was soon on his way to Edie Creek when news of the first rich gold finds leaked out. Mrs Pryke determined to follow him. She left on the Morinda *enroute* to the Trobriands, where her husband was to send a schooner to pick her up. But fate sent dengue fever instead, and added malaria for good measure. From Samarai Mrs Pryke was ordered back to Sydney. A second time she made the attempt. After a tempestuous voyage in the little Melusia she landed at Rabaul— and went down to gastric malaria. She was again sent back to Sydney. She made a third attempt in sheer desperation — and this

Papua New Guinea, 1930.

time succeeded. Mrs Pryke landed at Salamau when the only iron buildings were rough humpies hastily put together. P.P.'s store, an hotel (an iron shed with no accommodation, merely a storehouse and bar) and Mrs Clem Hendry's house. (She was the first white woman really to settle at Salamau.) The other few buildings, including a tiny hospital, were of native materials. This wee settlement was on the beach, with the gloomy mountains of the interior frowning behind. Mrs Pryke reached Lae aerodrome by a launch trip across the Huon Gulf, and next morning made her momentous flight to the Wau. Mrs Wisdom, wife of the Administrator, was the only woman who had up till that time flown from Lae.

Frank Pryke had come down from Koranga Creek to the Wau on numerous occasions expecting to meet his wife, but he missed on the rightful occasion and a native runner had to be despatched to him. When finally he did arrive Mrs Pryke threw her arms around him and just said: "Oh, Frank, get plenty of gold quickly so that I can have a plane!" "Well, I'll be blessed!" said Pryke disgustedly; "After all the trouble I've had getting down here you don't even say "'how d'you do?'"

On the walk up to Koranga Creek Mrs Pryke soon found that a skirt and shoes are not the clothes to wear when travelling along a Papuan jungle track and across boulder-strewn creeks. On arrival at the camp, Whizz-bang, the native house boy, superciliously eyed the torn dress Bind gave his lofty advice: "Lap-lap (skirt) no good longa this country, Missus. Tou wantem trowsis alla same master." And Mrs Pryke followed his advice as soon as she could get the "trowsis" and boots. The white woman, found herself away up in the Papuan heights, living in a house built of native materials, obliged to make the most of food that had been brought at the cost of 1/- per pound carriage (it costs 9d now) and with a handful of white men and hundreds of natives around her. Whizz-bang and Tulet (To-let) were the houseboys. Whizz-bang is a well known native character, cheeky, but very intelligent. This ex-head hunter has developed a mania for drawing. Whenever Mrs Pryke missed her writing paper she had simply to locate Whizz-bang, and he would be found drawing some miner or perhaps a particularly bloodthirsty-looking specimen of a kanaka. When he found out the use of a rubber he was in the seventh heaven of delight. "This little feller rub 'im make 'im go away altogether," he grinned.

Tulet was of the more sedate type plans its roguery quietly. Koranu, the real boy, was simply a heathen imp—but with a nasty line in impishness. One cheerful morning Koruna appeared in his noiseless bare feet at the living-room door, grinning fiendishly. Mrs Pryke nearly died. She had reason to—for Koranu held in each hand a big automatic revolver, and the unwavering muzzles were pointing straight at Mrs Pryke! The woman fixed the native with her eyes. She just glared while she tried to stop her heart from thundering. When she could speak she commanded firmly, "Koranu, put him piccaninny gun belonga Master back belonga room!" The cheerfulness fled from the boys face; he scowled with the quick sullenness of the Papuan. "Do as I tell you, Koranu!" the white woman almost shouted; "Quick feller now! Take him back piccaninny gun longa Masters room." She hardly dared breathe as she glared at the boy. She knew that each automatic revolver held eleven bullets, and her husband had told her that if a native pressed the trigger of an automatic he would held it there in fright until all the bullets streamed out! With no other weapon but her steady eyes Mrs Pryke threatened this gun-pointing boy with dreadful things, but he grew only more and more sullen—and still kept the guns levelled. She felt the inevitable would happen at any second. Then she took one firm step forward. Slowly, still scowling, the boy turned his back. Immediately the brave white-woman had him by the scruff of his neck and was soon relieving her keyed-up feelings by giving him "the father of a hiding." Panting and dishevelled, she flung him out of the house. By this time all her energy had been expended; so, locking herself in her room where no one could see her, she sought relief in collapse. But Mrs Pryke had not sought that distant outpost solely to make her husband comfortable. She took many trips along the mountain tops, seeking the jungle tracks and wading her way through rock strewn ravines in search of unoccupied country. She found it, too, at the head of Koranga Creek above her husband's and Les Jouberts leases. She took up thirty acres of gold-bearing country, but no sooner had she pegged her claim than she felt the urge of the gold fever — she must work the ground. Thus she experienced all the joys of battling against the usual Papuan difficulties. Boys must be secured to hew down the trees, to clear the ground, to cut water races, to shift stones, to dig, to carry, to work. These boys were finally recruited from the Markham River tribes. Mrs Pryke was soon "up against it." She found that to dig gold in New Guinea the miner must first have gold—currency gold—with which to start. Each boy cost her £27 all told. Then she had to pay him £2 per month, clothe and feed and house him, and send him, if ill, to the native hospital. She had to fight against many other worries, too; and she found out that sometimes a boy was not worth 5/, let alone £27 plus £2 per month and food that cost 9d per pound for cartage alone. She battled through, however, and finally had the satisfaction of proving her gold mining lease to be worth many thousands of pounds.

Frank Pryke, Joubert (Frank's mate) and Mrs Pryke got a nasty shock one day through the very queer reasoning of natives. A batch of Maree boys from the Upper Markham were recruited to work the claims. They were a weedy lot and much prone to illness. One boy in particular cost a lot of money and never did an, hour's work, so Mrs Pryke advised that he be sent down the mountains to the native hospital. She detailed off two of her own hefty boys to carry him, showed them how to make a bag stretcher slung between two poles, and packed them off with the sick boy. In a very few hours they returned "You put buy longa house-sick (hospital)?" inquired Mrs Pryke. " No got." "What did you do with him?' "He finish!" With visions of a dead boy and corresponding trouble with officialdom, Mrs Pryke called Whizz-bang. "You run quick feller now, see whether boy stop longa house-sick," she commanded. In an hour Whizz-bang returned laughing all over his face. "Boy stop where?" demanded Frank Pryke, "he die finish?" "No," answered Whizz-bang, "he stop longa creek. Boy leave him." All was explained! The sick man belonged to a different tribe from the stretcher bearers. When they became tired they had simply dumped him to die alone beside a quiet creek. Mrs Pryke loves the glorious weather and the excitement of gold-digging life on the mountain tops. There is no fever there when once away from the low lying coast. She is in Sydney now enjoying a well-earned holiday.

Adventure and Women in Lonely Lands

ION IDRIESS
Australian Woman's Weekly, July 1933

Real adventure falls to the lot of few women, hut Mrs. Frank Pryke is one. She has known the fury of a cyclone on land and sea, has flown over jungle-clad mountains, has bossed her own kanakas, and won gold under the roughest conditions in a primitive land.

Learning the ways and "talk" of brown and black savages, of securing and pre-paring tropical foods, has been an experience rich in educative and humorous value to this self-reliant, bright Australian woman.

She has just returned from a recent trip, a "civilised" venture this time, just to keep her husband company. He is one of the most famous of the surviving Papuan pioneers, and believes himself quite capable of looking after himself, but, of course, wives think differently from men.

She has put out from Samarai (Papua) in the ancient launch "Sorrento" with old-timer Fred Kruger at the wheel and several laughing Papuans as crew, and a Papuan girl as "companion." In boisterous weather she has passed along the beautiful Papuan coast, with the launch breaking down at regular and irregular intervals. On lucky nights she camped at plantation or mission station until they crossed the stormy Doibu Passage and beat up for Mapamoia.

Above them Ferguson Island, its black mountains running into the mysterious inland, the monotonous chant of a "sing-sing" coming from some hidden village.

The anchor going down with a splash and in the sudden silence a cur howling dismally ashore. Here greeted thankfully by Mrs Rich, wife of the Patrol Officer.

When Mrs Pryke called Mr Rich was away, as he is often for weeks at a time.

The young wife and baby are then alone except for a native constable, to listen at night to the muffled singing from the native village, the stamping dance of savage feet, abruptly broken sometimes by the menace of quarrelling voices.

A white woman needs something more than courage when she casts her life in these lonely places.

Only recently a native woman had been killed, and witchery, to avenge her death, was even now being hatched in the village. A feeling of sullen expectancy seemed brooding over the place.

There are only half a dozen white men scattered many miles apart around the shores of this large island. The natives, especially those inland, though leaving the whites alone, occasionally indulge in a little murder among themselves.

This sea-washed island, rugged and beautiful with its majestic scenery, will some day delight the eyes of tourists. What is far more, its hot mineral springs may prove wells of mercy to the sick.

The party cruised from point to point around the island, anchoring a week or two here and there, while Frank Pryke walked inland on his mining quest. Mrs Pryke, with the Papuan girl, made excursions of her own, visiting the miles of sulphur springs walled in by jungle mountains, with limestone cliffs all yellow-tinted from condensed sulphur fumes.

During a trip into the interior they saw a beautiful lake deep within the mountains, still and silent. Fish swam there, while deep pressed upon the trellised vinery at the water's edge were the tracks of wild pigs and men. In that brooding silence it looked a picture of peace. A truculent tribesman, though, warned them of a quiet water hole to drink of which meant death.

It is probably impregnated with arsenical mineral salts.

One blithe morning Mrs Pryke went singing to her favorite pool to bathe. She there met the largest crocodile on all the island, and her return to camp was a record.

GOLD-DUST AND ASHES

The Romantic Story of the New Guinea Goldfields

ION IDRIESS

The 26th illustrated edition now out from ETT Imprint, Exile Bay.

Brisbane Courier :-"His latest book is really the romance of the Edie Creek and Bulolo diggings, situated inland from Salamau; and with the discovery of the field are associated the names of diggers as "Shark Eye Bill" (William Park), Matt Crowe, Jim Preston, Arthur Dowling, Frank and Jim Pryke... men who in pre-war years, crept across the frontier, defying the Germans and dodging the head-hunters... These men endured terrible hardships, and frequently faced grim tragedy. Mr Idriess writes of it all, and writes of it as if he had been with them.. What a romance! What a story! It is packed with adventure, studded with splendid pen-pictures of pioneer prospectors, airmen, and patrol officers, and told with a fascinating simplicity that is borne from something very close to genius."

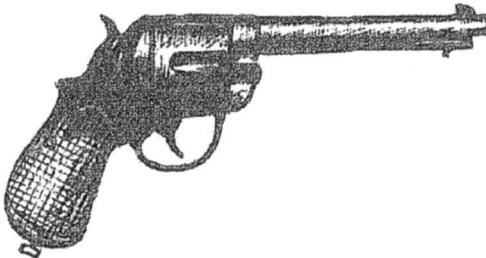

Frank Pryke's revolver, now at the NLA.

LASSETER'S LAST RIDE

An epic in Central Australian Gold Discovery

ION IDRIESS

The 45th edition now out from ETT Imprint, Exile Bay, illustrated with photographs, extracts from Lasseter's Diary and letters.

Morning Post (London):-"Perhaps the greatest of Australia's real life epics."

Daily News (Perth) :-"No grimmer tragedy than Lasseter's Last Ride has been recorded in the annals of our exploratory history .... Yet Idriess manages to keep his reader wavering between laughter and tears."

Otago Daily Times (N.Z.) :-"One almost finds it difficult to believe that the story is modern and true."

Sydney Mail:-"One of the most graphic, most poignant, and most absorbingly interesting tales that the chronicles of Australian exploration - those treasure stores of dramatic adventure - have ever revealed."

The Herald (Melbourne) :-"A true story that for sheer excitement, thrills, and sustained suspense, cannot be surpassed by even the most imaginative novelist."

The Telegraph (Brisbane) :-"This thrilling book reveals in convincing colour, the details of a story that is history and that has all the elements of stark tragedy."

Up the Creek

Edie Creek and the Morobe Goldfields

James Sinclair

Up the Creek
Edie Creek and the Morobe Goldfields

James Sinclair

Jim's last book published by Pictorial Press Australia in association with Arthur L. Jones OBE. Limited numbered edition of 650 copies only.

Contents:
Background Information Edie Creek Mine; Brief History of Mining Operations by New Guinea Goldfields; 100 Years Ago; British New Guinea; The Lakekamu; German New Guinea; The Koranga; The Interim Years; The Strike; The Rush; The Diggers; The Royal Commission; 1927; Enter The Companies; The Decline of Alluvial Mining; Deep Mining: Day Dawn; Deep Mining: New Guinea Goldfields Limited; Life On The Creek; The Phony War; The Italians; The NGG Strike; The Evacuations: Women and Children; The Evacuations: The Menfolk; The Bulldog Road; After The War; Edie Creek: The Twilight; Kaindi Repeater Station; Tony Heriot; The National Miners; Rikani; Edie Creek Mining Company; Niuminco; Reminisces and Reflections.

Order from:
Pictorial Press Australia, P.O.388, Corinda QLD 4075
Telephone: (07) 3716 0104
Please forward_____ copy/copies of "Up the Creek" at $45.00
plus postage and packing $15.00 within Australia = Total $60.00

Name:_____
Delivery Address:
_____

Phone Number or
Email address:_____
I am paying by cheque, money order or direct credit to bank account.
If using direct credit please use your surname as a point of reference.

Account Name: Pictorial Press Australia
Bank of Queensland
BSB Number: 124 028 Account Number: 11177226

www.ingramcontent.com/pod-product-compliance
Lightning Source LLC
Chambersburg PA
CBHW031005090426
42737CB00008B/684